when LOVE gives you wings

(tracking the evolution of love)

Gwen Editin

authorHOUSE®

AuthorHouse™
1663 Liberty Drive
Bloomington, IN 47403
www.authorhouse.com
Phone: 1-800-839-8640

First published by AuthorHouse   05/17/2011

ISBN: 978-1-4567-6405-0 (sc)

Printed in the United States of America

when

LOVE

gives you

WINGS

(tracking the evolution of love . . .)
by Gwen Editin

Foreword

Love brings with it such a myriad of emotion
when you move out of home at the age of 16
to begin living a life of "sin"
elope at the age of 18
are divorced by the age of 25
re-married at 28
widowed at 35
and re-married at the age of 40.
Love can be elusive.
Just when you think you "have it all"
it can disappear,
mysteriously reappearing in the most unlikely places.
This book was written to share a journey that
delves into diversity, but is
united by a single vision—to share, to re-create and to re-live.
Setting sail for that elusive paradise
to discover different ways
that we might fall and stay in love
it would be wrong not to share the passion
that can be forgotten, all too soon
when it is love that helps us to grow
and if we are lucky—we learn to fly.

Dear Reader:

Read this book as you would eat a piece of chocolate cake

Enjoy each tiny treasure, that you find within

Savour the moment, for its flavour may be fleeting

Men are not meant to live alone, they just think they can

Open your heart and your mind

"Neither" is not a choice

Dare to be wrong

Contents

when all I want

when all I want
is only you
I only need
that you want me too
if I could be "all"
that you would need
then I could show you
how love should be
to be everything
to love only me
to always be sure
that it's meant to be
no matter how long
it takes for us
to find what it is
when two people love
what tells me I "know"
this love is true
is that
all of my love
is what, I gave to you.

She knew

She knew that in a minute, he was going to pull her toward him. That should give her enough time to decide how to respond, except that suddenly she couldn't think.

From the day they had first met, Tammy had been hoping for this moment. Of course, she should have prepared for it.

Now she wasn't exactly sure what to do. To follow her heart without planning ahead, would be risking everything.

Tammy knew if she let Alex hold her, she'd want more. She wasn't sure if he was ready for that.

In the days following their introduction, she had tried to ensure Alex hadn't had much time to worry where their friendship might lead. They had slowly begun to know each other. Now all Tammy knew, was that she wanted him in her life.

It had taken months to build his trust. In past relationships, Tammy knew she had been more than a little selfish. But Alex was different.

Alex had a smile that conveyed such boyish enthusiasm, that he was incapable of deception. Or so it seemed. Still, she thought—best toproceed with caution.

Her instincts told her that Alex might retreat.

When he started to reach for her, her whole body ached to surrender.

Tammy still didn't know what to do, so she closed her eyes.

to touch

to touch your face, I close my eyes
you give me a kiss, and then you smile
of all the times, I dream of you
there's a way I hope, that you dream too
why did you come to me, this time
how don't you know, I want you for mine
when all that I feel, I give to you
so you can be mine, and we can do
the things I want, to be only yours
all the things that I love, about you are
all rolled together, into one wish
so you would see, and I know if
you could just feel, all that I do
there'd be no doubt, in your heart too
if you can't be mine
then I will ask you again
and I will wait for the day
that you tell me when
I'll take you in my arms
and then
I'll make you remember
and understand.

missing

missing always
the feeling of your arms
wanting you never, so far away
that I can't ever
hear all that you say
you asked me to share
what's in your heart
now I can't leave
the love that you started
when I only know
and remember your arms
I still need to know
the deepest part
I want the rest
of who you might be
to always be here, right beside me
so I'd hold forever
all that you are
you would then be, never too far
away from me, that
I can't hold you or touch
the memories you brought
to me with your love.

because I still

because I still believe
in all we're meant to be
and because you made me need
beyond, what one can see
much more than what I had
before
that now, I am still looking for
the way I felt, when you were here
that's only mine, when you are near
the way my heart feels
when you're home
so that I know, it's not alone
the things I never knew could "be"
if the words you said
were just for me
become somehow
a part of you
then, all I'd ask
is that you too
believe and know
so I'll be sure
in all my dreams
of the way things were.

how don't you know

how don't you know, all that you are
this love I feel, that makes me sure
the way I love, goes far beyond
what I can see, or anyone
would ever know, or dream could be
all that I know
is how I feel
if you only knew, you'd understand
the boy I love, inside the man
the certainty of how I need
could only mean, that you're for me
when all you are, is just one man
who made me want to take your hand
you showed me things, I've never known
a love that I, could call my own
if you could see
my love, inside
all that I feel, but not know why
you'd see you are
all that I want
all that I need, is what you've got
and just as surely as I breathe
you'd know that you, were meant for me.

the memory of what

love was before –

is to hold the hand

that wants to be yours

Tammy opened her eyes

Tammy opened her eyes once she realized Alex hadn't reached for her.

She thought she had heard a sigh. Was it a sigh of regret or something else?

So much for reading the male mind, from the way their hands moved.

His were just as still as if he didn't know he had arms.

Could she have been wrong about the way he felt?

Her mind went back to their first meeting, when Alex had taken her hand. She had tried not to look too excited, although she felt her smile widen once he spoke her name.

"Nice to meet you, Tammy, " he had spoken in a quiet but firm voice.

She thought he had held her hand an instant longer, as if he wanted to get to know her better.

Someone used to getting his way with women, no doubt. Yet who could resist that friendly smile?

Tammy was hoping he would see her differently. Thinking back now, no doubt all women who met him thought that way.

That was his charm and he knew it.

Tammy told herself to stop dreaming, and to answer his question.

"Everything's fine," she replied. "is the work on schedule then?"

if you

if you would only love me, the circle'd be complete
I wouldn't need, to seek and find
or to hold you, in my dreams
I wouldn't care, the way you laugh
had kept me, company
I wouldn't think, you here with me
would be all, I really need
I'd keep the way, you looked at me
that made me, start believing
I'd have the things, you told me
that I'd begin, to feel
if only, for just one more time
you'd look at me, and smile
I'd know the way you left me, is
still something, that was mine
to always be, forever yours
for as long, as I could dream
yet when I speak, my heart's the one
who says, that it still needs
when I remember, what we shared
I only, want that back
for when I dream—I know it's meant
I cannot yet, forget.

I close my eyes

I close my eyes
to see you smile
I wonder where you've gone
and while
I think of you
more than I should
I wonder now if perhaps
I should
try to love and live
without
so you'd be free to go about
and I wouldn't have
to tell you too
all the hopes
and dreams, I had for you
but then we'd never
know just what
or for how long
we'd have this love
the love I have
that will not change
the other ones
just not the same.

I pull you close

I pull you close, to have you near
our spirits touch, now that you're here
when first we met, somehow I knew
you'd be the one, that I would choose
I loved the way, you held my hand
it felt so right, but even then
I didn't know, what love could be
until I saw, the world you see
you made me feel, how flowers grow
you taught me things, I didn't know
for all the times, you cared for me
I knew that you, would always be
a friend for life, my other half
you taught me tears, and how to laugh
and through it all, right by my side
you let me know, that you would try
to bring me all, that you could bring
a song for me, that you would sing
that what I'd need, you somehow knew
they were the things, you needed too
from this day forward, we will be
the best we can
now that we're "we".

when first

when first I saw you, all alone
I wondered, whether you would know
I was the one, you were to find
so I could claim you, all for mine
when first we met, I thought I knew
but now I see in fact, there's few
to find the love, that we have now
the way you made me feel, somehow
I'd often wondered, if I'd find
a special someone, to be mine
but your arms held me, so close to you
that I could hear, your heart beating too
the eyes that smiled, so softly then
brought light to make me see, that when
God sends us friends, so we can grow
until that time, we cannot know
unless that special someone, comes
to bring with them, a special love
so I ask you then, to take my hand
"together" is, what we should plan
the hands we hold, are not our own
but only know, they're coming home.

if we could dream
together

just like the way

I remember my
dreams

from yesterday . . .

Just as he started to reach for her

Just as he started to reach for her, Alex realized that Tammy had closed her eyes. When did that happen?

Alex had pictured being able to catch a whiff of her perfume, but now he stopped his hands midair. Closed eyes could mean so many things.

He didn't want to make a mistake. Tammy was different than other women and he wanted to be extra careful.

His mind went back to the day Alex first met Tammy. After he shook her hand, he was reluctant to let go. He wasn't sure if she could sense his ambivalence. Perhaps she hadn't felt anything at all.

So he recited the usual "nice to meet you" and tried to focus on the conversation at work. It was hard not to gaze at her a bit longer.

Alex thought, if he had learned anything from his past . . . best not to overreact. For today, it was probably a good idea to do nothing.

He wrestled now with a thousand questions, but reminded himself he had decided to let Tammy make the first move.

Alex forced his hands to drop to his side.

He bit his lip and asked "is everything okay?"

if

if I were to see you, just one more time
would you then know, you were meant to be mine
could you tell me you loved me, just like before
would you tell me, you never stopped caring
and more
dreams that you left, for me to hold
I'll keep them here, until you come home
I know in my heart, you'll always be
the one that I love, and so I will keep
saying a prayer, that you'll understand
when I think of you, I remember the man
whose love is the kind, I've never known
whose heart is the one, I want to own
the smile that you gave, is something that I
will keep in my heart, for the rest of my life
and if you knew only, all that I feel
you'd come to know, how easy to steal
my heart away, from where it was hidden
I'd left it where, it wouldn't be found—then
the heart that you took, you should bring back
so we can love, "together" at last
but until I can hold you, and never let go
the love that I keep, is all that you own.

if I tell you

if I tell you, that I love you
would you then, have more to say
if I show you, how I love you
it'd be more, than yesterday
I know that you said
you couldn't surrender
but the way that you held me
is what I remember
eyes that were dark, and shining with light
I think I know why, your hug felt so right
let me be the one, to stand by your side
I know you could love me
if we had more time
no longer meant for someone else
if it's the same love, that I have felt
that could be us, if you agree
it's something "meant", for you and me
to share and treasure—forevermore
the love we both, had known before
if you would let me love you
I promise to be that
and if I could, I'd bring you more
than what you've ever had.

the way

the way that I love you, is something that
will live through all time, so that you'll know when
this feeling of love, that is never gone
something you know, that will carry on
part of your heart, for the rest of your life
now has a reason, to give me your light
I needed your arms
and you were right there
almost as if, you knew I'd be here
waiting so still, to give you my heart
to tell you how we, should never part
but all of you, is what I want to know
because all of me, is what you now own
when did it happen, I'm still not certain
but feel and believe, it was meant to—then
all that I want, would be only if you
told me, my love is what you needed too
when I see the man, I know you to be
I'm just not sure, if you'd ever need me
but I thought I would ask, just in case you can see
the love that we share, gives your life meaning
the same way that I, remember your touch
I'm hoping you'll tell me, that you also love.

how did you

how did you manage, to capture my soul

why did God, give you to me

why is it now, that all I can do

is remember you, in all my dreams

you said you loved me, then you smiled

and in that moment, what I felt

was every dream, I've ever kept

though memory says, it won't forget

if you let me hold you, one more time

and allow your heart, to love mine

my love for you, could live on today

here in my heart, it would always remain

and if you held my hand, in yours

the way, I remember from before

tomorrow would be "yours and mine"

with all my dreams, and then enough time

for me to seek and find out just

who it is, I've grown to love

the memory of you, and all you believed

all of your hope, and dreams that I need

if I listen to what, I keep in my heart

the things that I hoped, you would say

if it's meant some day, that you'll be free—I could stop dreaming today.

my heart says that

it wants to wait

it only needs

the love you gave . . .

Alex expected Tammy to reply

Alex expected Tammy to reply with some personal detail about herself.

She ought to know that he was interested in how she was, not just what she was doing.

But the way she had asked if work was 'on schedule', took him aback.

It was evident by not being too personal, Tammy wanted to return to the business association they both relied on, and not pursue a closer friendship.

Why had he thought she was different than other women he had met?

He couldn't let his disappointment show. Alex decided instead, that he would make it clear that her response was the one he had expected.

The coolness in her voice felt like a slap to his face, so he replied abruptly with "okay, back to work then."

Alex was so busy thinking about the other night, that he didn't see the look of disappointment that crossed her face.

He heard her say "okay, see you 'round then".

Tammy turned quickly on her heel to leave.

And then she was gone, before he could say another word.

whatever

whatever I can "do", let me "say"
whatever I can "say", let me "show"
whatever you want, let me "be"
there's nothing more, that I could feel
let me hug til I'm "through"—I want you to see
all of the "everything", that you are to me
just like the pebble, that starts the wave
I'll always remember, how much you gave
I want you to have, more than you thought before
could ever be yours, and just to be sure
you understand all, that I want you to have
I'll need to check, if you have other plans
close to my heart, is where you shall be
forever and always, a part of me
you are a man, who needs to be told
that in my eyes, you will never grow old
for beauty and kindness, come from within
all that I know, is how much you have given
things that you said, that you'd like to bring
"whatever" I need, so that only means
each day that we love, I will treasure it more
for each day we have
is one more, than before.

I am

I am helpless and homeless, until you return
there's nothing more, that I can learn
my heart holds a place, that only you
can fill as completely, as what you do
there's never a choice, when there's a delay
for the love that I want, you're the one I await
while I wait for your heart, to slowly reply
I already know, the love that's in mine
you brought to me, honesty and trust
so I could never, say "no" to your love
you brought me flowers, for every day
they never grow old, but what they say
is how much you care, and think about me
and in return, I'll never be free
I only want and desire, to be what you need
and that would be everything, you brought to me
more happy my smile, more peace I have found
I have to tell you, you make the world round
now that I've met you, my heart has declared
all that I seek, is here and right there
when you make me feel, all "is"—as should be
there's no more I can say, except let it be "me".

in the quiet dawn

in the quiet dawn of morning, I wait to see

if maybe today, you might come to me

with the sound of your voice, perhaps you would be

coming to tell me, of the love you now bring

when I feel your love, it pulls me to you

and I wait in the shadows, of what looks like two

hearts that were heavy, now bright with hope

certain with knowledge, of the love that they know

but for now, I must wait—until I hear too

you're coming this way, to bring me to you

to where I've been waiting

for all this time

until you could tell me

that your heart is mine

the song that I hear, goes on and on

it talks of "forever"

and even beyond

so now I must look

for the face that I love

there's a love that I keep, and that I'm sure of

I'll hold it for you

until you arrive

and I can love you, for the rest of my life.

I wait

I wait for you now, to come back to me
never too sure what to dream, or believe
I hear my heart speak, but I cannot prove
why is it that, it needs memories of you
if I listen to what, the echoes declare
I'd need to know, if you'd meant to be there
but it's here in my heart, where you belong
I looked for you then, but the wind was so strong
it blew on the hope, I've always kept
I'd find some day, that you had come back
the sounds of the wind, carried whispers of love
those are the things, that I now dream of
though spirits may wander
mine's never too far
to look for wherever, it thinks that you are
the closer and nearer to you, it can be
the more it can understand, why it should feel
that never again, will it pass this way
without thinking back, on "our" yesterday
the time that we met, was when I had meant
to tell you I knew, that I'd never forget
for the dreams I have now, they bring me to you
and in the end, they bring your love too.

if I can't give you

the key to my heart

it's because

you already have it

When Tammy got back

When Tammy got back to her office, she picked up a message to go see him. What now? She sincerely hoped Alex wasn't the type who would make her account for the other night.

She was determined not to be just another trophy, but it was hard not to remember how she had felt lying next to him.

Hadn't her mother always told her trust no one, especially a man the night after. What had she been thinking? Of course that was the problem.

Tammy hadn't thought further than how sweetly Alex had smiled at her.

Must it always be like that? Were there no men in this world who could be trusted—or was it, that she always picked the wrong kind of guy . . .

But Alex hadn't seemed "just like the others." She had noticed how polite he was, treating everyone with respect and kindness. Perhaps that was the problem, Alex was just being courteous. She had been swept away by his manners and now she was no different to him, than the others.

Tammy arrived at his office and Alex waved her in. She sat down, her heart beating just a little bit faster from the uncertainty of what was next, or maybe just from seeing him there. There seemed to be a lack of expression in his eyes, which made her nervous. Tammy couldn't afford to make another mistake. She held her breath and looked at him quizzically.

This time, Alex looked closely at her when he asked—"are you sure everything's okay?" Not sure what to expect, Tammy decided to play it safe.

"Yes, I'm fine" she said.

Although she had hoped Alex would want more of an answer than that, she wasn't about to volunteer anything without being asked directly.

if I captured

if I captured your heart
to keep it for me
would you then let me
do as I please
if I write you a note
to explain it's my way
to tell you I miss you—and any day
I can't touch your face
or feel your hand
makes me more certain
that you'll understand
when I say, that I love you
what that really means
when I say, that I need to
be sure how you feel
all that I know, is what my heart says
now that you're gone
I know that it meant
looking for when, love will bring me to you
I'll never leave, if you "promise" to
not ask me how, but only "how" lucky
it was the day, you said that you loved me.

as your voice calls

as your voice calls to me, I remember it—then
I need to know, when I will see you again
if we could just sit, together at last
and hold each other, like we did in the past
to share more dreams, of times that we'll have
when and if only, you can come back
still waiting for you, I have no choice
but to see if perhaps, your heart's also both
feeling the love, that I have for you
or living a life, that is "just waiting" too
if you take my hand, I promise to be
whatever you want, and all that you need
as you are to me, all that I'd ever
want for the rest, of my "all of forever"
I wait for you now, since you had left
I hope and I pray, that you won't forget
with your arms around me, to keep me near
that's all I need, to bring you here
right beside me, is where you will be
while I still wait, so you can believe
the love that you sent, keeps me content
but only until, I can see you again.

you've touched

you've touched my heart, in a way no one else
has ever done, or that I have felt
each time I think, of your embrace
I think of all the different ways
you held me up, so I could see
much more than what, I thought I would need
when you put your hand, over my own
I felt something then, that I've never known
love entered my heart, and has never left
it brought me a light, I can't forget
the closeness I felt, the bond that I know
now to be, the beginning of growth
just as a flower always needs rain—some
turn their face to the warmth of the sun
I could then feel, how you gave me a part
of yourself, but now—it's there in your heart
is the one place I want, to know I belong
or my love for you, will just carry on
all on its own, looking for what
you gave to me, in letting me love
if I can't hold you, it would be the same
as knowing that, I'll never see you again.

in the early morning

in the early morning dawn, I find a place
to remember the things, I saw in your face
the way that you love, the caring you showed
they always will be, what I want to know
to ask for something more, I protest
would be asking for something, that doesn't exist
the "more" that you gave to me, now I feel
the "all" that you gave, should be all I need—still
you'd have to be me, to know what I mean
and only if you, have my heart to see
how love can bring light, to all that was dark
then you took my hand
to give me, a part
so I'd have no choice, but to always be
"eternally yours", by what I should keep
still captured by love, a power that you
may not even know, all of its truth
it carries on, with a life of its own
for those who can feel, the light you have shown
I should say only, I always will
be prisoner to what, you gave to me—still
always, forever and even beyond
my love for you, was meant to live on.

no need to talk

of the love we had

all I need to hear

is that you can't forget

Alex couldn't stop feeling

Alex couldn't stop feeling that he'd made a mistake with Tammy.

Something was wrong and it was up to him to find out more.

Perhaps he hadn't been thinking clearly when he left the message for her to come and see him. If things got difficult, he could change the conversation by discussing their ongoing project. That might work better.

Alex thought they had such a good friendship. Tammy had always been so easy to talk to. But perhaps it was his role in the project that had interested her more, and they didn't know each other as well as he thought.

Damn those women who keep a man guessing! He didn't like the feeling of being used, when it was obvious to him that he'd been honest.

Tammy probably knew exactly what she was doing.

In fact, it was his mistake to have called her. Whoever said it was a man's world. Why was it up to him to make the next move?

Alex was berating himself for thinking they had something special, when she arrived—a little breathless.

It had been like that from the moment they had met. Tammy had a way of making him want to protect her. But maybe he had been all wrong.

Alex didn't appreciate the thought of having been used. He hesitated, trying to read her expression. He wanted her to look at him before asking,

"Are you sure everything's okay?"

Again, there was that coolness in her reply. "Yes, I'm fine."

It was the kind of answer that meant 'don't ask me anything else, please.'

So he decided not to say anything else, except "see you 'round then."

From the look on her face, they both knew that was a dismissal.

whatever I am

whatever I am, you have made me
you were the one, who made me believe
in what I can do, and how I can love
you found a way, and you have touched
a part of my heart
meant only for you
I needed to know, just what you do
when you opened my eyes
to feel how much more
my life came to be, much more than before
you gave me your smile, so that I would feel
how flowers grow, and that they are real
the colour you brought, to my life then
became what I live for
but until, and when
I hear your voice, and can hold you again
I won't dare to breathe, unless in the end
I stand by your side, and I feel you near
then my heart knows, that all of "it's" here
the "it" that it wants, and needs—to live
has something to do, with how you have given
when you were here, and I felt that touch
all I could say, was "yes" to your love.

I search

I search my heart, to find what I need
and in my heart, I find there's one dream
that you're meant to be, a part of me
still
I know I must wait, to see if you will
tell me you love me, and that in fact
you know in your heart, that you love me back
how long that may take, I don't know when
and until that happens, I can only wait—then
if you were to say, you want me too
I'd have to tell you
that I knew I'd love you
the moment you looked my way
and you smiled
my heart gave a sigh, that took me a while
to understand all, that it would feel
it couldn't allow, my love to reveal
all that I wanted, when it's only you
that it now needs, for love to come through
so as the sun shines, and the moon glows
if you see those things, then you will know
the love that I hold, and it was "meant"
you'd be the one, I can never forget.

just one more hug

just one more hug, would be just fine
I want you to know, that they are all mine
I was waiting to see, if maybe you
could do all those things, like you used to do
if you could just hug me, as if you were mine
I promise you that, it won't be the last time
if I could just have you forever, with me
I'd never ask for another thing,—see
no one else before you, has done
the things that you, and your love have come
to bring to my life, that I can't forget
so many things, that we haven't yet
begun to explore and find together
I think it just may, take all of forever
we need more time together, to find
more ways to see, how you should be mine
more love to share, than you've ever known
more ways to find yourself, as no one
before you, has made me want to remember
how it should be, when you surrender
the way that it feels, when you're in love
how suddenly life, can be all that you want.

I was just

I was just getting back to sleep

when all of a sudden

I began to need

I wanted to see your face again

I needed your arms

to remind me when

the way that you held me, had felt so right

that I only want, to shut my eyes tight

I would open my eyes

if I knew I would find

that you have come back

to say you'll be mine

that you need me too, as much as I want

that you want me, but in a way that you've not

ever believed, could come to you in your life

and that now you've found, the reason why

but only if you, have found you belong

here in my arms, would it be wrong

not to be able, ever to know

where love could take us, so that it could grow

into the love, that I know you could feel

if you've ever known "need"—and remember me "still".

if the words are mine

but only come to me

when I think of you

then who do they belong to?

Tammy hoped

Tammy hoped she hadn't given anything away by the expression on her face. She had been told many times, people could read her like a book.

She still had her pride. Or did she? What kind of person would shut down, and then want to answer a simple question with a million of her own.

Her mother had always told to take a deep breath before speaking.

Just in case one changed their mind about what they should say. As a matter of fact, sometimes silence was a better option.

Tammy repeated that advice to herself as she dialled his number.

Yet something told her she had to talk to him. She owed herself that much.

Tammy heard a familiar "hello?" as Alex picked up the phone.

Just the sound of his voice still had such an effect on her. Tammy shook her head, glad that Alex couldn't see her hands trembling.

"Can we talk?" Tammy asked.

His reply gave her stomach a knot. "Not now, I have to go . . ."

"Okay then, later?" she wanted to give him another chance. Or maybe she meant, give herself one last chance. She hoped he would let her explain.

"Sorry, I'll be out of town for a few days. Don't know when I'll be back." Alex's voice sounded strained.

Tammy closed her eyes & sighed. You should know better she thought.

Some things never change. And some men never change either.

"Okay." All she could think of, was "talk to you later then".

Tammy heard the click of the phone as Alex hung up.

And to think she had planned to ask him to hold her again.

you must

you must have sent love, to me last night
because in my dreams, you hold me tight
you held me, so I couldn't breathe
and that I'd know, you needed me
the way, you made me feel before
is now, the love I'm living for
you made me feel, how you must care
and in my dreams, I have you near
during the day, you take my hand
at night, you're here with me and then
you hold me close, just like before
to make me sure, there's nothing more
that I could want, or ever seek
except the way, that you loved me
the way you gave your heart, so free
is something that, I'll never feel
until I hold you close, to mine
the same way that I know, I'll find
a world you made, the warmest love
for what you did, was "hold" and touch
a deeper place, inside my soul
where dreams can live, and I now go.

you lifted

you lifted me, out of the dark
so I could see, into your heart
a different world, where only love
can live within, and then you touched
your soul to mine, so I would see
you are the one, who was meant to be
a different love, that this time I knew
would only come, when I'm with you
your eyes could always, make me see
and I only keep, what you gave me
you took me to a place, where I
would like to live, for my whole life
so now, the only dream I have
is that we'll be together, at last
as if I've been waiting, all this time
for someone like you, to come into mine
I thank you now, for making me dream
and for the kind of dreams, that you bring
I have no doubt, the way it was
was meant, to teach me how to love
but there's something else, you did to me
that now, I only live for my dreams.

it's in

it's in my dreams, that you need me

and in this dream, I make you see

that we can say, all that we mean

then you tell me, that you believe

heaven sometimes, will send us love

that we before, knew nothing of

how God above, will perhaps say

tomorrow is bound, to yesterday

the seeds you planted, now bear fruit

the flowers grown, have taken root

the branches of the tree, now stretch

beyond where we thought, lay the edge

the largest tree, that stands so tall

becomes the way, that shows us all

to see beyond, the highest hill

so then we know, that what we—still

are searching for, has all this time

been something, that we'll only find

when we have learned, how love should be

and how it's meant, for you and me

to hold our hands, together for

a love that we, both knew before.

as much as

as much as I try, I don't want to forget

you are the reason, that I have yet

to say all to you, that I meant to say

if you could have stayed, it was yesterday

the day you came, to say "good-bye, I'm leaving now, but I will write"

more flowers bloom, where we stood once

they mark the spot, where we found love

then days became nights, the skies went dark

and I knew then, of just how far

away from me, that you had gone

and all the days became too long

I wanted to say, that I remember

except for the way, that I had never

thought I'd love—has come to me

and now I only want to dream

for my heart to say, it would give you up

it never wanted you, so much

as when you said to me, that night

"just let me hold you, one more time

I will be back, but you know that

for surely, love is all we have"

but the nights grow cold, so I ask when

it's meant to be, that I hold you again.

when you live in my
heart

it can't be too much

to tell you again

how much you are loved

Alex watched Tammy

Alex watched Tammy for a moment as she left his office. Then his phone rang. He had told his secretary to hold his calls. What now?

Alex was pale when he hung up. Something had gone wrong with his dad's operation. He had been asked to go to the hospital, just in case.

That sure changed his priorities. Before the phone call, he was mulling over how to handle "her".

Alex thought he knew Tammy well enough that he could read her.

But it felt like he had been shot down. More like he had just been shut out.

He would have liked to know her reasons. Maybe she just changed her mind.

Not being sure what his next move should be, Alex had been shaking his head when the phone rang. Now he knew exactly what he had to do.

He had to get to the hospital, to speak with his Dad one last time.

Alex was reminding himself to drive carefully, when the phone rang.

He realized it was Tammy, but his mind was already elsewhere.

"Hello?" he said, hoping this was one time she would get straight to the point. When he heard her say "Can we talk?", he didn't have time to explain, but only managed to say "not now, I have to go."

He barely remembered explaining he'd be out of town for a few days.

Alex wished he could tell her more, but what was the point right now?

Alex thought he had heard Tammy sigh before she hung up.

He drove off, hoping she would understand and that he'd have a chance to explain later.

He also hoped that his Dad would be okay, until he got to the hospital.

I don't

I don't want, to remember
how it feels, to surrender
arms that held me tight
and made everything "right"
I don't want to believe, in love anymore
unless you can tell me, what love is for
I don't want to feel, what I felt with you
when you came to me, to pull me into
wherever it was, that we were going
somewhere between, a start and a growing
a hunger that searches, for what it needs
a thirst that can only be quenched, when you feed
the heartache of knowing, that you have missed
something, you'd never mistaken for this
feeling of how, it would be right
if ever, you came to me in the night
the night brings me dreams
but then morning comes
and when I awake, I know you're the one
whose arms that I need, I must live without
whose kiss was so sweet, it left me no doubt
don't tell me again, about all that you feel
I know what we had—perhaps all too well.

I will wait

I will wait for you, because I need
the love you brought to me
a special love, that we both know
when someone lives, inside your soul
you're really only, half of "who"—when there's another part of you
two spirits joined, in thought and deed
were always, ever meant to "be"
I need the light, I know I feel
the way your smile, warms me to see
the choice was never, mine to make
when you touched my heart, it walked away
I turn to your light, to where I "became"
then I found out, I won't be the same
what we have now, and what we had
I felt from the moment, you took my hand
if you could just tell me, that you have heard
what your heart says, that it has learned
I will wait to see, if your love's coming to me
my heart doesn't mind, it will never be free
never free of the bond, that binds me to you
it found a true love, that was more special too
and when two become "one", they can't have 'enough'
when all they know, is how much they're in love.

I turn

I turn to the light, I suddenly see
I feel the warmth, that you bring to me
it reminds me again, that I am alive
it's a gift that you have, when you arrive
among things I've learned, more since you came
all that I know, I'm not the same
more happy my smile, more blue the sky
a sudden knowledge, of what I should try
to feel what it is, to love every day
to know in my heart what we found
and I pray
I am the one, who has loved more than once
for each time I see you, I fall in love
captured by you, leaves me no will
I always feel only, my love for you—still
for all this time, and all through the years
I gave back to you, all that I feared
I hoped that my love, would keep you safe
I know that my best gift, was my own faith
content with the knowledge, that we once loved
is the one thing in life, I'll not have enough
but if I am able, to just let it be
more blessed to give, than to receive.

I can feel

I can feel you, and I hug you back
my love for you, is something that
whatever we shared, it stayed with me
and it's as constant, as the tree
the tree that becomes, a forest in time
so love began, and it tells me that I
will not walk this path, the same way twice
for you are the reason, I watch the time
just as a father, loves his own son
my love for you, goes far beyond
beyond what I see, or what I can feel
past the time that we had, and it always will
be something that "is", and "was", as should be
of all the things, that you brought to me
more peace to my soul, a hand I could touch
the way you made sure, I could feel all your love
the song that is never ending, goes on
the words that I write, are those that keep coming
we can't always hear, when words are unspoken
but I'll always feel, the love that I know
the faith that I have, the love I 'believe'
are the best blessings, that I could receive.

your return,

is all I need

to bring an end,
to all my dreams

so I could touch,
and feel the way

it was back then, on our last day.

The next morning

The next morning, Tammy checked her machine for messages. Nothing. Looked like she was going to be on her own this weekend.

Rather than stay in the city, she decided to drive up to the family farm. The only problem with that, was that she'd have to see her mother.

But it was a beautiful fall morning and the sight of leaves changing colour might brighten her frame of mind.

Something about driving past cows grazing lazily on grass helped her to relax. But it also made her miss having Alex's company.

She remember how he had always been willing to listen to her before.

Perhaps she had been a little hasty in assuming the worst.

Tammy began to remember all the little things he would do, that had made her trust him right from the start. The way he'd always look right at her when she was talking. She realized that's why she had assumed he could read her mind. He'd always been so easy to talk to.

Tammy had to think carefully about what had happened, to make her mistrust him. Looking back, perhaps it had been her fault, not his.

At least, she should have explained her thinking and given him a chance to respond. Tammy realized he couldn't always read her mind.

Suddenly she wanted to talk to Alex, but was there going to be a next time?

Tammy was still debating whether to call Alex again and leave him a message, when she arrived at the long dirt road leading up to the farm.

She'd better concentrate on driving safely, instead of daydreaming.

Besides, she was too far out of range to be able to use her cell phone now.

I travelled

I travelled in time . . . back to when you were mine

I had wanted to ask, if you'd hold me

then to dream of the days, when I'd hoped that we

would share all our lives, whatever we had

and I could tell you, all I wanted to—and

no longer looking for that, which I need

because I had found it, with you and—for me

you had a way, of knowing my heart

you need only smile, but I find it so hard

today, to remember—just what it was

that made me fall, so completely in love

perhaps it was just, the way you would laugh

or maybe it wasn't, as simple as that

it could have been, that I gave you my heart

it wanted to know what it'd feel like, if far

so far away from my own—it would be

where it was loved, and it felt so free

it needed the warmth of the way, that you'd turn

to look in my eyes and teach me—I'd learn

I wanted to know all the things, that you would

I stayed in your arms, for as long as I could

I didn't feel alone, when you left the first time

because I thought I could dream, and go back in time.

I'm still

I'm still in love, with the way that you are
but I haven't a clue, what you've done to my heart
to make it so that, it needs only you
and then how it only, wants what you do
the love that you gave, and the caring you've shown
those are the only, things that I've known
I can't explain, all you've done for me
except that I know, I will never be free
each morning I wake, I feel all your love
at night when I sleep, I remember your touch
when I hear a voice, that reminds me of you
I look for the face, that I've grown to love—too
but it's more than what, I can tell you I "know"
there's something else, I can't describe it all—so
I can write all I want, but I'll never be
able to show you, how much I have needed
my soul rejoices, for having found
the one who I know, whose smile has a sound
there was a way, that you'd never complain
so then I could only, love you again
for who you are, and all that you do
I'll always only—love all of you.

if you make

if you make me yours, I want to be all
that you've ever wanted, to be in your arms
take me as I am, and change me to be
all that you seek, or will ever need
I want to be only, what you have dreamed
so that you'll know, the power of believing
the same kind of power, you've given me
I want for you, so you can be free
you've brought to me, so many things
I believe that you must
have been hiding your wings
I trust in the path, when you lead the way
I would follow you, to the end of "always"
sometimes one must wait, for the future to bring
more than we asked for, and then everything
that we ever sought and searched for, so long
love brings to us magic, and then we belong
toward the light, and away from the cold
if you listen to hearts, you will find that they show
when the one that you love, is right beside you
it's not just your heart, but it's in your arms too
when love is right, what then comes through
not only hearts, but love surrounds you.

if I wrap

if I wrap your arms around me, like a blanket of love

I feel your love surround me

and I remember your touch

my head is looking, for a place to find

where it can rest, for all of its life

my hands want more, than what they thought

was coming my way, when last I saw

my eyes still search, the open skies

to look for a sign, of "just" you and I

I know I still feel something 'left'

which means I can't forget

the love you left, lives on in me—in ways, I don't know yet

it makes me smile, it holds my hand

it helps me to be "more"

if ever I think, that you don't care

it reminds me, of "before"

so when I ask, where are you now?

you live on, inside my soul

the things you did, the words you left

all things, that I should know

so I wrap your arms around me, and then—just like before

I know, that what you gave to me

means, I'll only want you more.

those we love

are not lost

when they live on

in our hearts

Alex arrived at the hospital

Alex arrived at the hospital just before visiting hours were over. But nurses were expecting him and they took him directly to his father's room.

The hospital smell reminded him of the last time he had seen his mom. Mom had never told him just how ill she was because she hadn't wanted him to worry "about nothing". Although he had never been able to tell his mom, he had felt cheated. Mom had passed away the summer he had hardly visited, much too busy setting up his own business and often too tired.

Alex wished she hadn't made that decision for him, and he realized that it still bothered him. He didn't like the feeling of living with regret.

Alex was more than happy to see his Dad raise a hand to greet him. Dad's handshake wasn't quite as strong, but it was still his trademark.

"No one needs to fuss over me," he said. "I'm getting better already".

Alex was relieved to hear his Dad's voice. He was even more relieved that his Dad believed he was going to be okay. Or did he really think that?

Alex was going to ask about that, when his Dad said, "Well, I'm glad you came anyway. It's always a good thing not to leave loose ends. Did you have anything to tell me, perhaps bring your friend to visit me next time?"

Alex had just been thinking about "her". Perhaps it was his pride that had prevented him from probing a bit more. He should have made that extra effort, although he felt that he shouldn't always be the one to ask questions.

He'd have to think about Tammy a bit later. Right now, he wanted to be here for his Dad, while he still had him. Alex was still pondering when his Dad said, "there's something I want to tell you about your mom."

you reach

you reach for me, and I hug you back
a thousand times, I had pictured that
we'd find a way, to seal tomorrow
and then I'd never, have to borrow
from what I know, or I can recall
I wouldn't have, to dream at all
I'd have my own life, the way I thought
I wouldn't have 'need', or even want
my wish for all time, forever—"hereafter"
that
I'd be able, to hear all your laughter
I'd keep the dream, that I dreamt to
be "that" one, who you would run to
unlike the leaf, that falls gently down
my feet would never, touch the ground
but just like the branch, is part of the tree
I'd reach for you, and find that you're 'me'
or at least, I could hold any part that I want
since all parts of you, are what I had thought
I'd ever want—to have, or need
our love would come, and make you believe
in all "hereafters" and 'evenmore's
then what we'd have, would be more than before.

what a gift

what a gift, you've given me
to see more things, I've never seen
to think of things, I never thought
that I could think, or that I'd ought
to dream the dreams
you brought my heart
to know, you'll always be a part
to know the sounds of love, that you
had given me, so I'd know too
to hear the words, you didn't say
to know your heart, responds the way
I wait to hear your answer, that
shows my heart, it's home and yet
today, has been another day
again, I hear the things you said
they echo always, in my mind
and are the ones, that I still find
when I go looking for you, there
I always feel, how you are near
I know the love, that you have sent
makes me more, than I've ever been
and I still feel, the way you touch
the one I know, that I still love.

to see

to see the sun and not feel its warmth
is to look for you, and not hear your voice
this I knew, when I was in your arms
all this I felt, from the way that you are
if once again, I could feel your touch
I would again
fall completely in love
if we could sit together and talk
if we could hold hands, or go for a walk
shoulder to shoulder, or hand to hand
touching and feeling, within our hearts—and
our innermost secrets
we could exchange
knowing our love, will not ever change
for we have a bond, that will last for all time
I know that I'll always, want you in my life
when I find that your love
stays with me still
I feel how my heart, has its own will
if I look for the sun, to find that you're gone
I know without doubt, it would be wrong
to let go of my love, and my dream from before
when I will love you forever—perhaps even more.

make me forget

make me forget, what it was like
when you and I, were side by side
help me remember, for all of my life
what it felt like, to hold you that time
the sun gave its glow, to my heaven on earth
and I held you tighter, as if I should learn
that never again, would I have you near me
closer than "that", to be sure I would see
the way that you smiled, when you looked my way
every time that you laughed, I felt joy again
you looked down at me then, as if to say
let me at least, love you for just one day
if even for just one time, in my life
let me enjoy you, right by my side
we knew we belonged, together in part
for if we had decided, to listen to hearts
we would have never, said "goodbye" to
the love we shared, and the love that we knew
although it may seem, that "always" is too long
it means to me, not enough time for one
when "two" is what's needed, to make love complete
the way that your love, has made me feel.

if I were to say

I believe in love

I would have to tell you

that I believe in "us".

As Tammy drove up

As Tammy drove up to the old farmhouse, her stomach tightened. She knew her mom would be asking more questions about Alex.

She wished she hadn't been so confident things were going to work out. She had already gushed about all the things she loved about him. Her mom had said Sarah had never been so excited about a man.

Now what was she supposed to say? Tammy sifted through various excuses for the fact that she had decided on this visit at the last minute.

If she could only figure out what her next step should be. As she pulled up, her mom interrupted her thoughts. "well, aren't you a sight now."

Tammy must have been frowning, although she had promised herself to stop doing that. She could do with less frowning, more smiles all around.

Tammy remembered Alex telling her to try a different approach by asking her mom for advice on something.

"Mom, can I get your opinion on something?" Tammy asked.

That seemed to work. As Tammy could see her mom relax, she hoped she would have a chance to thank Alex.

Tammy then realized she had learned to feign coolness, whenever there was an awkward moment. Suddenly she felt ashamed. She would have to try and make up for it next time, no matter how little pride would be left. She hoped Alex was the forgiving type.

It was time to grow up, no longer the right thing to hide by pushing people away. She smiled and marvelled at how mature she felt now.

She looked up and saw her mom smiling back.

if I want

if I want to give you, what you brought to me
how do I make you, feel the way that I "need"
the hand that you held, no longer free
it only remembers, how yours made me feel
my shoulder then looked, for the right place
where it could rest, so that it could make
a home of the way, you brought to me
a love that I knew, only from dreams
and did you know, when you stole my heart
that all you'd leave, would be a part
the part that you left, to belong to me
now plans to leave, and just wants to be free
to run to the one, that it knows as its home
now that it's found, all that you own
more of the feelings, that it wants to feel
so many ways, you helped me to heal
all of the things, it has never known
except to be sure, that now I will owe
you—more ways to feel, how to be loved
with no end in sight, and if that's not enough
it needs you to "be", and wants only you
the way that you are
how you do what you do.

something

something you do, when you bring the sun
that shows me only, how you are the one
something that happened, when you arrived
that tells me that, you are part of my life
if all you have, to give to me
is just one day, I will then be
more happy to have, and grateful to know
that for one day of my life
your heart, I could own
until I can hold you, and feel you again
I'll always need you, right to the end
so if you remember, all that I get
from loving you—and never forget
love only comes, once I've made you mine
and so I must wait, until the right time
no end is near, to the way that I "need"
I only want you, to know all I feel
if just one day, a lifetime could be
I accept, if that's all you have for me
this time I promise, I won't run away
then we can always, ask love if we 'may'
for if it is meant, that love will stay
I could love you forever—and for all of "always".

how

how can one hug, last so long

to make me feel, that I belong

how can one squeeze, be so tight

and at the same time, feel so right

perhaps it was, in the way that you looked

that all of my breath, is what it took

away from me now, towards you—its home

like a bird flying south

to what it knows only

as the key to surviving, the cycle of life

like a mother who bears, her child until birth

like the salt and the sand, that make up this earth

a reunion of sorts, of two parts that were

separated somehow, meeting again and now sure

to discover each other, is how it was meant

the ways that they fit together, and then

now reunited, at last they would know

to enjoy a love shared, is a dance that should grow

a chance to become, all they should be

returning to live out, all of their dreams

now understanding

the true meaning of home

and once they've arrived, no longer alone.

I must have

I must have known you, from before
that's why I need you
so much more
in another life, a previous time
we had a love, when you were mine
the way I love you, feels to me
the same way, that I need to breathe
the way I know, your arms can feel
your smile, your kiss—are all so real
that's why I missed you, all today
I must have loved you, yesterday
I feel the love, I have for you
is something, that you should know too
have you forgotten, what it was like
to want all day, and through the night
if you don't recall, the way I do
I will have to try, and reach you too
how love can be, all that you need
when you want your other half, to feel
the way your heart, knows that it loves
it only waits, for that next touch
now standing here, I hold my breath
when all that you gave, I can't forget.

when Love is right

it can

live on its own

Alex's dad said

Alex's dad said "we had a bit of a scare there. It got me thinking. I don't want to leave things, like your mom did. We had disagreed on how much to tell you, but that was the way she wanted it. Right or wrong. She did what she thought was best. She did want me to tell you how much she loved you, not to hold it against her. Just wanted you to know."

His mom and dad had always been opposite in nature. But Alex had seen how that had worked for them, creating a kind of balance.

His dad continued, "life is sometimes too short, not to speak your mind. You have to learn how to listen to your heart. Sometimes that can mean speaking up when you're not sure. The point is that when you're not sure, that's exactly when you should be finding out what you can be sure of. No point in spending your life guessing. No point in living with regret.

His Dad looked at him pointedly. "Don't take this the wrong way, but today made me feel like I should say something. Just in case there comes a time when I'll be thinking to myself—I should have spoken out."

"Don't be afraid to test yourself, so you'll know what to do each time. I've seen many times when you shy away from confrontation. That doesn't make sense, when I know you're capable of handling conflict. You're better than that. The more often you do this, the better you'll get at it. Don't be too proud. I'd rather see you pursue the truth and live with certainty, than to run away from confrontation. Because then, you never will never find out just how close to the truth you were. That's a long speech coming from me."

Thinking it over before bed, Alex decided he should call Tammy in the morning. What gave him courage, was that it was the right thing to do.

the hand

the hand that reached, for mine in love

held more for me, than just your touch

it beckoned to my state of mind

it dared me to discover life

it brought compassion to my soul

it made me feel all this, and more

then bondage, becomes more than willing to

follow the one, whose heart is pure

not asking for, but giving forth

more love, so that you know there's more

for a heart that overflows with love ...

is one that might just fill you up

no longer hungry, you become

a force united, not just "one"

no longer searching, all the world

but to live each day, filled with purpose

let me be the one, to hold you until

you know in your heart, that you are loved—still

so you learn what it is, to be loved every day

I give you my dreams, from yesterday

to become your tomorrow, "forever" you'll keep

no longer alone, but all that you'll need.

your smile

your smile, became a laugh so loud
the faintest whisper of that sound
awoke my ears, as if to know
to cling unto a tiny hope
that you would remember, what it was
that made us fall, so much in love
it wasn't then, we were so sure
but only when you'd left, we heard
the sound of emptiness, within
the echoes, when that loneliness wins
when suddenly, your partner's gone
you understand, why parting's wrong
my heart said that, it couldn't see
unless that was a smile, for me
nor should it ever, be so wrong
to want to feel, that we belong
a bird must find, its nesting place
the wolf still roves, to find its mate
so on we go, if search we must
but home, is where our souls had touched
and for one perfect, moment in time
I could tell the world
that you were mine.

his eyes

his eyes that smiled, a little sad
they tell the story of love, once had
once full, now empty they became
still waiting for love, to come again
what is it, that was "meant to be"
why is it that, I feel the need
to touch his face, with both my hands
to keep the smile, he showed me—then
there was a time, his heart belonged
he told me once, there'd been someone
the love he thought, was his to keep
now taken back, now gone to be
the smile, that bravely sets out to
show the world, what it can do
it only needs to find its home
to know that it, won't be alone
inside my heart, I keep a place
for the man I know, I'll love always
waiting to see, if we belong
I hope some day, to be "the one"
to keep forever, all for mine
until the clocks
run out of time.

I had dreamt

I had dreamt for so long, about the "right one"
I knew at the moment, when love had begun
it makes you remember, all the small things
about him, you love and then everything—
the world and its people, all come to be
not as important, as he was to me
if he only knew, the way that I feel
he'd understand, the hope that I keep
the love that I wait for, so wait if I must
because he's the one, I know I'm to love
I felt in that moment, when he looked my way
I knew in an instant, the words that he'd say
suddenly as if, I'd known him before
I knew what he'd say, would make me want more
I don't need to be told, he's meant to be part
when I already know, how he lives in my heart
some part of my soul, that was missing—now found
when he took my hand, the stars turned around
when stars are lined up, and God smiles on us
hearts can then open, to hold much more love
for the hand that reached out, to touch my own
was the one that I knew, was for me alone

love tells me

that you alone

hold the key

to my coming home

Suddenly Tammy felt shy

Suddenly Tammy felt shy. How could she ask for advice without giving too much away? Anyway, she had mixed emotions right now.

Perhaps that was the key. She had always prided herself on her ability to analyze first, then make decisions later. Her first step always, was to decide exactly what she should be thinking. Feelings are for the heart.

The best thinking should be with one's brain. Analyze the facts, then decide what she should be feeling—apart from not wanting to feel foolish.

Maybe that was part of the problem. Growing up with a constant fear of not wanting to be taken advantage of, she had put up barriers to expressing her true feelings. That, and a false sense of pride.

After all, why was it so important to be able to "keep" her pride? What was the purpose of "pride" anyway. Was there any point in trying to "keep her pride" if she really didn't have a good reason to mistrust Alex. In fact she realized, she was the only reason not to trust in him.

She hadn't given Alex a fair chance, in not acknowledging her own baggage. Wasn't that how most couples have misunderstandings?

Tammy felt relieved, it was so clear to her now. Why hadn't she seen that when she was looking right at him. She felt an urgency to explain now.

That is, if Alex was still willing to talk with her. With that thought, Tammy resolved that next time would be different. She was a changed person but she'd need to prove it.

Her mom's next query interrupted her. "What was your question?"

what have you

what have you done, that I don't know
what I should feel, or tell you to go
why can't I say, what I should do
when it's my heart, that says I need you
as part of my life, what I live for
not that I want, to need—any more
I don't want to be, so helpless in love
I don't want to feel, that it's too much
to want every day, and all through the night
to feel in my heart, that you're my life
all that I want, to understand this
is to find why I love, and know what was—"is"
that I should love you, was meant to be
what makes me love, is how you make me need
perhaps I can't fight, what's meant to be
perhaps I should just, let my love "be"
to live on its own, it only needs you
then I should know, all I have to do
is hold you forever, close to my heart
know that you're always, meant to be part
forever and always, I'll remember your touch
and let my memory, bring me your love.

my place

my place is there, right beside you
and I know, that you can feel it too
at least, that's what I thought you meant
when you told me, that you won't forget
the way it felt, when we first touched
that told us both, it must be love
or was it only me, who knew
the way that love, can feel so new
the time before, when you had looked
that extra breath, I thought you took
or was it mine, that I had caught
then calculating, what it's not
it's not, that I've felt like this before
or that I knew, I'd want much more
it's not so, that I knew that you
would be the one I'd want, but—too
it seems forever, that I've known
the way that love's, already grown
and yet I know, I've never held
you in my arms, the way it felt
when I imagine, what love could be
if I could only, keep you with me.

the place

the place I go, to hold you close
it tells me, that I love you most
more than I thought, I'd ever feel
or was it meant to be, just me
when it was only once, we met
but I knew then, I won't forget
I'll find a way, to make you say
you meant to say, you loved—that day

until I know, you also feel
that special love, I want "to be"
for if you didn't, know it then
I need to make you, understand
and however long, it takes for you
to say how much, you love me too

I need to wait, to see if you
will find the path, I'd chosen too
not that I knew, that I would be
re-living that day, in memory
but for what I want, I'll wait until
you understand, the words "I will"
I'll wait 'til then, to hear you say
you loved me then, and still today.

I only

I only need, to close my eyes
to bring to me, the way you smile
with my eyes shut, is how I keep
the love that you, had given me
the words I know, you meant to speak
so I can then, tell you I need
no longer "one", unto myself
I knew that, you were someone else
I can't explain, just what it meant
to hear you call, my name again
the way a bird, calls for its mate
that somehow knows, it will be fate
that shows a heart, how it should choose
before you even, thought you knew
how can it be, that you would know
to make me love you so much—though
I wasn't sure, how love begins
until I felt, your heart within
when flowers bloom, then multiply
the way I feel, my love inside
that could just mean, we're not the ones
who then decide, what love becomes.

it takes a

special person

to listen

with their heart

Alex reached for the phone

Alex reached for the phone first thing in the morning, then hesitated. It was so clear to him last night, but now he wasn't sure exactly what to say.

Know what? Maybe just start with a "Hi, how are you—can we talk?" Alex suddenly realized that were Tammy's exact words when she had last called him, although her voice had sounded rather tense.

But this time Alex told himself, he would ask and not just guess at what was bothering her. He'd have to act on his resolution to be more direct. Less speculation, more clarity. Above all, don't be afraid to be honest.

Speaking of honesty, he really should tell her he felt differently about her. There had been something special whenever she was around, that touched his heart in a way . . . well, no wonder he sometimes didn't know what to say. He'd rather hold her, than talk. He gave a sigh.

Alex dialled her number and got the machine. Where had she gone? Normally he would have expected she might have told him, but he had to admit he had kind of brushed her off.

Alex only hoped there was enough trust between them, that Tammy would give him a chance to explain. Although sometimes, loving someone should mean forgiveness. He wondered how the word "love" had come up.

For now, he could only hope she would understand. Come to think of it, when he had taken the time to give reasons for his decisions at work—she had been pretty accepting.

Alex continued to rehearse what he'd say next time. He decided it was time to be honest with himself. He needed to tell her he wanted another chance to work things out, no matter how strangely she might look at him.

I knew

I knew, I could always hide in your arms
the way, that you kept me safe from harm
I felt the strength of your embrace
it kept me warm, so I could face
the world outside, would never be
too much to bear, for you and me
I'd have held you longer, if I'd known
that you were never, coming home
and I'd have hugged you harder, than I did
if I knew then, all that I'd miss
eyes, that remember all they've seen
ears, that never told their secrets
hands, that held my heart until
it knew the way home, but then—and still
my heart once weary, now can smile
rejoice in love, and all the while
my soul, once wary of its heart—now finds in fact, it plays a part
and if I thought, I would see you again
this time, I'd keep all the words that you said
if I tell you, I know I couldn't love you more
I think you would find, that unlike before
I can't love you more, than I already do
for the way that I loved, was meant for two.

what was it

what was it, that you tried to say

when you held me tight, on that last day

was there something more, you wanted from me

so I would know, I'd never be free

all the memories, of the times we had—echo so loudly that now, I can't

ever forget the way, my heart

keeps telling me, we should never have parted

else run the risk, of no return

from that secret place, in my special world

the place I go, to be alone—with memories full, of you and only

time, can bring you back to me

if I could live in the past, I'd keep

the way I felt our love before—but I didn't dare to ask for more

if "more", was what I knew I'd need

I'd have kept you here, to be with me

now all alone, and so I must—carry on, without your love

learning to live without a heart, can be

something, that also sets you free

free from the way, I need your touch—never to want to be in love

always to wait to have you near—now I won't need, to have you here

to say the things I need to know—to hold me, so I know how close

our hearts had been, when we had touched

heaven on earth, when we had loved.

whatever I do

whatever I do, I take you along
you keep me company, wherever I've gone
the warmth, you brought me
a bright sun, so I'd see
the moon that allows me, only what I'm to keep
however long it takes, whenever it might be
I will always and forever, want you only for me
what can it be, to always want
looking forever, for that other part
searching for ways, to show you my love
I can't only say, that I live for your touch
from the minute you came, and gave me your hand
from that day forward, I'd understand
not only the way, you would care for me
but all of the things, you made me feel
living "forever", in both of our hearts
a life of its own, which makes it not hard
to say that I'll always, love only you
and to tell you this time, I know I'll be true
for the feelings that come, when you're with me
live on in my heart, and I'll never be free
of all that you gave, so no matter 'when'
I'll wait by the road, until I see you again.

next time

next time I won't say, that I believe
in love that was meant, to be only for me
next time I'll know, I won't forget
all that you gave, and that you left

each time I say, I can be strong
now that it's clear, that you're really gone
what I do know for me, there will never be
someone like you, to watch over me

the way that you cared, like no one else
has ever done, or that I have felt
the words you said, the way you smiled
live on in my heart, and all the while

I look for you, to cross my path
I need to know, if I will see you again
you didn't say, when you'd return
from that, I know that I should learn

so often, we can't control our lives
but must wait to see, if only we'd try
when we first met, I thought we'd be friends
not knowing then, about love without end
and if I've been wrong, about being alone
you made me feel, that I'm coming home.

listening to the echoes

of a heart that still loves

how don't we know then

what's "not enough"

Tammy looked up

Tammy looked up at her mom who was still smiling. She had never seen her look so happy to give advice. Maybe because she had never asked her for any, before.

She heard herself ask "Do you think it's too late to change someone?" What her mom said next, surprised her.

"What makes you think you need to change them? Perhaps it's you, who needs to change first . . ."

"What do you mean?" Tammy replied.

"Well, think about it. Every interaction we engage in, is a reaction to something we have done or said. The result is a function of what we initiate."

Suddenly, Tammy was glad she had resolved to be more open. The "new" Tammy was already making changes in her life, beginning at home.

"You know you're right. I never thought of it like that" Tammy said.

"Just remember that it's often too late to change a first impression. You know that old saying "Plan as if you're going to live to be a hundred—but act as if this could be your last day on earth? The "key" to living a long life, is to try and say what you think. Nothing eats at you as much as regret over things unsaid. Within reason of course. You don't want to hurt anyone over something like your own silly pride, right?"

Tammy could only agree. Why hadn't she asked her mom for advice before today? She should have known she could count on her. It had only been her own 'silly' pride that had prevented it. That was now a thing of the past. Tammy decided she should work on her future and also the "new" her. That meant listening with her heart and telling her brain to take a back seat.

thinking of you

thinking of you, I am never alone
and loving you, feels like I'm coming home
my heart looked to rest, so weary from what
life had been bringing, to make it stop
it wanted to feel, no more of the way
the love that it lost
that lived yesterday
but needing the peace, it finds with you
with all that I feel, not sure what to do
for loving again, may bring back more pain
when I had thought, I would not love again
why risk all the heartache, that love can bring
except for the way, you make everything
all wise and all knowing, not wanting to stop
the feelings of love, that you have brought
but to let love be, all the things that I need
to let wonder and joy, come back to me
I'd have to say now, that I believe
the love that you said, was "meant to be"
perhaps if I were, to try and escape
I must then turn, and tell you again
but the hope that you bring, I can't deny
when the memory of love, stays on my mind.

this time

this time I'm helpless, to flee from the way
my memory returns, to our yesterday
the day started then ended, with all of my love
just waiting and hoping, that you would touch
my heart once again, like you did before
a dream that I had, now I'm living for
the gentle encouragement, your smile always brought
so I could dream, and I would have not
only one dream, left to sleep on—that I'd awake, and you would be gone
as I wake in the morning, looking for you
my heart sleeps in the night, and then it dreams too
the dreams that I have, are mostly about
living with love, and erasing doubt
no more to wander, it knew that it's home
once you arrived, no longer alone
the 'oneness' it feels, the closeness it needs
when you came to me, then it could feel
no one before you, has done this to me
all that you gave, what my heart has seen
and so—on and on, the circle of love
reminds me today, how only your touch
is all that I ever, dreamed I would need
and if you were here, I could believe.

I may not

I may not be clairvoyant, so I can't tell you when
but I know I can tell you, the same answer again
each time I think, that I can't love you more
I find that I've learned, to love you more than before
if the colour of love changes, as it grows large
mine would have been, all the colours there are
and if you could hear, the sound of a smile
the one louder than yours, could only be mine
I never imagined, one person could teach
all that you have, but still out of reach
are all the dreams, you gave me to dream
and all your ways, I've grown taller to see
more ways to love, to know how to care—then
I just need your return, to let me know when
the sky turns to blue, no longer dark
and the clouds that rolled in, know to depart
if you could be me, for just one day
you'd know all the love, that my heart contains
but only for you, will it open again
for you are the one, who made love the same
so if ever I find, I haven't learned
I'll remember the love, you gave in return.

those we love

are not lost

when they live on

in our hearts

Alex went to check

Alex went to check on Dad, and to say goodbye. His Dad seemed to know he was feeling anxious to get back to the city.

So Alex wasn't surprised to hear him say "looks like you got some things to take care of. You should get back to them. I'll be fine. Now that we've talked, I feel much better."

Alex knew he would remember the look of contentment on his Dad's face for a long time.

In the meantime, Alex could hardly wait to get back to see Tammy. He had tried calling just before he left, but still no answer. Alex decided to drive a little faster than he usually would. It felt urgent to see her again.

As he drove, he reminded himself—'from now on, live each day like it might be your last'—say what you're thinking. That way, no regrets.

Alex smiled to himself. He was more at peace, thinking how it was the right thing to do. How good it felt to "know" what to do. That's how honesty can change you.

He suddenly felt very humble. His Dad had ensured his "loose ends" had been taken care of. No matter what happened, he would be at peace for speaking his mind. Now he expected that Alex would do the same.

"I won't let you down, Dad" Alex whispered to himself.

if I could

if I could stretch time, to make it fit
it still wouldn't hold, all my love in it
for the way I feel, stretches far beyond
what I can see, any end of
it keeps me closer, than I should be
a prisoner then, is what you've made me
so willing am I, to do what you want
I only want now, if you haven't got
I'll take it for you, to give it away
I need to be sure, that for today
you understand, how I feel all our love
something my heart, found with your touch
the time when the sky, had opened for us
so I would know, there'd be not enough
time to show you, all the ways one can be
held as a captive, as you do to me
so all that I ask, is a little more time
if time is enough, to make you mine
I need to fit, into one small space
just enough time, to caress your face
until I am tired, of keeping your heart
right beside mine, a light in the dark.

you said

you said you loved me, then you smiled
and in that moment, what I felt
was every dream, I'd ever kept
though memory says, it won't forget
I'd love to live, the dream instead
of wanting back, the time we had
the way you held my hand, in yours
all that I ever wanted, was "more"
and if tomorrow, could be mine
I'd ask again, for just "more" time
the time I need, to find out just
how it is, that I should love
if I can't show you, all the love I keep
perhaps I should learn, to show you a piece
so if tomorrow, becomes our yesterday
I wouldn't know, that your love's gone away
if you could hold me, one more time
then tell your heart, to love mine
my love for you, could live on today
it would never leave, nor be exchanged
for in my heart, will always remain
all of the love, that I thought you gave.

you make me

you make me dream, like no one else
never before, have I ever felt
the "all" that you, have made me feel
so I'm not sure, of what is real—
the heaven, that is in my heart
or what I felt, when we had parted
the joy I feel, deep in my soul
that comes whenever, you stand close
the countless times, you reached to hold
the many ways, that you had told
me, all the loving in your eyes
whatever it was, that you decided
when you gave your hand, to me in trust
so I could feel, "never enough"
the love we have, will always be
the kind that makes you, trust your feelings
and in return, I can only say
take "all" I have—for from today
I know I'll never, love again
my heart gives you, the only claim
to everything, I've wanted to feel
from the way that you
shared all your dreams.

I only have one heart,

not two –

and that was the one

I gave to you.

my eyes

my eyes stayed wide open, to see the face I love

if only you could feel, how I love and long to touch

I felt the way you held me, and I remember that was when

I always thought that what we felt, would happen next time—then

if somehow it will come to pass, that you could not return

I only know I would have said, teach me—so I'll learn

to live my life without the one, who makes me want to laugh

show me how to be at peace, without my other half

help me to decide again, which way my life proceeds

when all I want to learn right now, is how to never need

I never wanted you to know, how much you mean to me

I thought it best to tell you, that I really just can't see

why I should care, if you're not here—it's really just the same

except the way, I remember now . . . the way you called my name

so I listen close—in case my ears, can hear all my heart had said

but I really shouldn't listen much, before I go to bed

for in my dreams, you come to me—to tell me that you love

that all you want to do right now, is remember that last touch

the one where I had held your heart, so it could not escape

and what you said to me that night, was . . . do not be afraid

for I will always be with you, to guide you through what's next

and if you don't mind telling me, "you know I loved you best"

I could leave your side and not return, so you would not forget

for the way we loved, was all my heart—and it has never left.

let me be the one

to show you my love

so I can believe

in all of my dreams

somehow the knowledge

Somehow the knowledge that she should follow her heart, gave Tammy the courage to pick up the phone.

After all, she hadn't actually heard Alex say "it's over".

She hoped he'd be home, but her heart sank when a recorded voice directed her to leave a message.

"Hi Alex—it's me, Tammy. Sorry I didn't let you know I was out of town for the weekend. Let me know when you have a few minutes to talk. I'll be here."

Tammy's stomach felt a little upset, but she felt the weight of past indecision suddenly lift. She should be able to get to the bottom of what Alex had been talking about, by asking exactly what he meant.

How easy was that really. It seemed logical now that she had talked to her mom. It should have been on her "must do" list rather than a "perhaps later" one.

Leaving behind an imagined slight, was a relief. At least, she hoped so. Replaying in her mind the many times Alex had come to her aid in the past, led Tammy to a strong belief that she had misjudged him.

"Pre-judged" him, was more accurate. Until there was some concrete evidence that she could not trust him, she should rely on her instincts. That meant no preconceived perception that Alex didn't care about her. That also meant no assumptions based on her own bias. That meant being willing to face the future, without anticipating the worst.

The knowledge that she wasn't going to hide anymore, gave Tammy a warm feeling. Whatever it was, it was a new beginning.

if I could only

if I could only, understand your love
perhaps then I'd learn, what is "more of"
to have more of, what I've always wanted
to feel more of, why you haunt me
to know more of, what I really need
to see more of, to truly believe
to have more of, all I'll ever
want today, and then forever
to love you more, than I would ever do
to love someone, as if I always knew
the love I have, would have been
my loving you, for all you did
although you said, it was "nothing" really
all that I know, is what I've been feeling
the "more" I love, the less I need
and "all" I gave, I should give for free
if I could learn, all that you know
I'd be able to find, the "more" you know
you made me dream, the way you do
and I've grown to feel, the same things too
for "hope", is what you made me see
and "love", is what you brought to me.

perhaps

"perhaps", is such a lonely word
perhaps, could be "not" having heard
so "maybe", would be better—then
than all the dreams, I haven't dreamt
"maybe" means that it's possible
for dreams that "haven't", to be—still
to become reality, in time
of course, I would dream that you'd be mine
if only, for the shortest while
and at least then, I'd have your smile
locked away in memory—safe within my heart, it'd be
always mine for me to see
and love would be, within my reach
you'd be the one, who'd want my love
and all I'd need, would be your touch
for me to say, I knew that you
wanted to say and tell me, too
you felt the power, of what we had
take on a life, which was bigger than
no ordinary love, this is
that grows, because I dream "what if"
for love that's true, lives on wherever
for those that know, we'll love "forever".

when love means

knowing

that you'll be forgiven

Alex was just coming in

Alex was just coming in the door when he heard the click of the answering machine. He didn't stop to check who might be calling him, but immediately dialled Tammy's number.

Something told him she had been trying to reach him.

He was glad that she picked up right away. No more games.

Alex took a deep breath "Can we get together for coffee right now?" He had promised himself that he would tell her what his Dad had said about having no regrets. He wanted her to understand why he had had to rush away. He needed to explain more about his resolutions.

In fact, there was a lot more explaining he wanted to do.

"Sure" Tammy replied.

He thought she sounded different, not as tentative as in the past.

"I have a few things I want to tell you—first of all I had to go see my Dad. I didn't tell you he was in hospital, but he's okay now. Talking with him made me realize I have much more to share with you, than I have been."

Tammy could hear a certain relief in his voice, and she responded, "I've also been doing some thinking, and I owe you an explanation for . . ."

Alex cut her off. "You know what, I don't think you owe me anything. As a matter of fact, I'd like to start all over again. First, I want you to know that I really care about you. Don't ever think I don't."

Tammy replied with "your place or mine?" She began to tremble when Alex said "I'll be right over". But she reminded herself there was nothing to be afraid of—for honesty brings with it, a special kind of courage.

my heart

my heart wants to know, how you do what you do
and why would it be, that I love only you
I've said all I can, I can't say much more
except that I love you, more than before
it crept up on me, it entered my heart
now it won't leave, even when we're apart
the love that you left, so I'll never need
the way that you smile, lives here with me
so now I can dream, and just like before
I hold you in my arms, and then—more
more dreams come to me, so I become
a prisoner of all, the love that you brought
for you captured my soul, and left no escape
so how would I ever, want to leave you again
if ever you need me, for anything at all
just call out my name, so I can respond
right now all I hear, is the song in my heart
the one that began, the day that we parted
it beckons to me, and holds me close
it tells me to wait, for the love that I know
how we found each other, the day that we met
is what I'll remember, and never forget.

who

who steers the ship, when it goes adrift
the compass that lives, within the heart—fits
it seems to know, when the course is awry
though not always quick, to know reasons why
it knows in the way, when it feels wrong
to continue sailing, the path it is on
the wind may then shift, to pull it aside
to tell it to look, for the way that is right
a journey begins, with just one step—and until it is home, will never end
it travels along, until it can feel
and only rests, when it's found meaning
the search continues, until it is sure
that it has found, what it's looking for
the feeling of peace, of having arrived
the way that I feel . . . with you and I
that which makes sense, of what in our lives
reveals an answer, to all that we've tried
so in my heart, I look for that peace
the one that I know, you brought to me
it came to me then, and I look for it still
if only I knew, you'd return to me willingly
as discovery unfolds, what our hearts need
I wait to see, if you come back to me.

if only

if only in my memory, perhaps it is enough
to know there was a time, when I had my own love
"perhaps", is such an "only" word
it really doesn't help
for "only" happens, when I dream
and then like ice, it melts
the image fades, and you are gone
then here I am, wondering how long
how far away, you must be then
for you to not have called me, when
last we spoke, I thought that you
had meant to say, you loved me too
I knew the words, but did not speak
in case the love I had, was "need"
I'd search the world, to find you still
I only need one dream, that will
bring you back to me, so I
could hold you near, so I can try
to understand, why I should need
to love you more, than I can speak
I'd hold you longer, one more time
but only, if I know you'll be mine.

if this is a dream

teach me

to believe

Alex lived only

Alex lived only about a fifteen minute drive away from Tammy, yet it seemed an eternity before he was parking his car.

On the way over, he started to list the points he wanted to cover.

First, he wanted to erase any doubt that she might have, regarding his feelings. While he couldn't predict the future, he was willing to work at better communication.

He wanted her to trust him, and to feel comfortable. He needed to reassure her that whatever Tammy wanted from their friendship, he was willing to try. And that he would make time to talk things out.

Alex realized that his feelings for Tammy had brought about a change in him which felt good. Wasn't that what love was all about?

Wanting the best for someone else, in turn brings out the best in you. Recognizing that for once in his life, he had stopped worrying about how things might look or "what if"—Alex felt a new kind of calm.

Alex resolved to listen to his heart, instead of putting his pride first. That made him certain that his actions would be the "right thing." Besides, he knew if he didn't try, he'd live with regret. He didn't want to live like that.

As soon as Tammy opened the door, Alex took her in his arms. He put a finger over her trembling lips to stop the tears as she looked at him.

In an instant, Alex had decided there was a time for action and a time for talking. Right now, words would not be enough.

So he kissed her instead.

when someone

when someone loves you, like I do
you only know, what it's like to
feel my heart beat faster, when
it feels you near, and it knows then
how love can hold you, in its grasp
not knowing, just how long it's meant
that we should love, until the next
time we see each other—and
to live for only, just your smile
to want your hand, to hold mine while
if hope could live, for longer than
it needs, to keep the dream we have
then hearts would know, they only need
to share the dream, that they believe
and all at once, they'd have once more
the love they had, that they lived for
when first we met, I grew to learn
my only dream—that you'd return
to find the love I had, I still
keep the dream, I'd had "until"
for I would kiss you, if I knew
that this is what, you're dreaming too.

let me

let me be the one, to hold your heart
let me be the one, who takes on the part
if you would allow me, to wipe your brow
I could tell you I love you, no matter how
the many times, I call out your name
and you turn around, not knowing the same
the same one who stands by, to watch you sleep
I am the one, who has always needed
to tell you, you're loved and forevermore
each day I lived, I've loved you more
I'll always love you, no matter what
you can't or you won't, but haven't forgot
you're here in my heart, where you belong
the place where I go, whenever I long
to remember your touch
and the way that you held
all that we shared, and now I can't tell
you more than I've said, again and again
I know that I'll love you, always the same
no matter when, no matter how far
no matter how close, or how far apart
because one heart can only, hold what it knows
and all that you gave, was more than I'd hoped.

Yesterday, I did not know

Yesterday, I did not know meeting you—would change my life.
Today, I give thanks for the way you shared yourself.
Tomorrow, I will still be celebrating the joy you have brought to me.

Yesterday,

Today,

and Tomorrow—

I will remember all that you have taught me and
I rejoice in the difference one person can make.
I wish you each and every small joy that is possible . . .
somehow, you always knew how to make things grow.

I am helpless

I am helpless in your arms
I still dream of your charm
those eyes, so full of love and care
the "all", you wanted me to share
the "more", you brought to me
the "now", that you have made me see
there's a "before", I never knew
except for, only just too few
times, I've felt a special love
that begins with how, only you can touch
some inner part, I never felt
before we met, and now I melt
the thought of what, our love could be
"all" that you can, and make me see
the "more" I know, that you can bring
how 'only' you, would be everything
the "all" I've ever, wanted to feel
is what, you've come to make me need
but I only, want to start again
if you return, to hold my hand
just like when, the earth was made
I can't forget, all that you gave.

if

if you want me, I am yours
if you need me, I wanted you for
all of the things, you did for me
whatever it was, you made me feel
you made my heart, grow bigger still
the way it feels, when it has no will
because my heart knows, its other half
whenever it hears, the sound of your laugh
if anything, should stay the same
I only want, that your love remain
although it's not always, safe to 'want'
sometimes in life, it's as if we ought
the "want" no longer, what is left
but only what, I won't forget
no need to ask me, to forgive you
for all you thought, that you didn't do
I forgive you for all, that you haven't done
except for the way, I know you're the one
whose love I will say, was always meant
to be mine to have, and make me feel blessed
the price to be paid, I must accept
when loving you means, I can't forget.

God made you

so special

there

could only be one

of all

of all the reasons, God made me love you

there's nothing wrong, that you can do

whenever it rains, you bring the sun

the flowers all bloom, because you're the one

who opened your arms, to hold me there

and I found a place, that keeps me where

I feel so safe, I won't run away

I would just like, all of my days

to be full of the way

I remember your love

to keep the memory, of your gentle touch

the arms that know

just how to hold

the way that I want, to never grow old

until you are here, right beside me

so I can touch, and hold all that I see

the face that I love, the man that I know

the reason that I, am able to grow

as the butterfly finds, the way it was meant

to carry her safely, toward her own heaven

I need to be sure

you want only me

and that I am also, your reason to be.

when

when I'm missing you, I hug you back
never quite sure, what to do next
then I remember, all that you brought
into my life, and I know that I ought
to give more thanks, for while you were here
I never wanted for anything, dear
were the words, you gave to me then
and all I could do, was count the days when
you brought me more love, than one heart could hold
for me to keep, until I grow old
you held my hand, and then my heart
so I would know, the day that you parted
how it can feel, to be so in love
I only live, for the moments we touched
the need that I feel, to see you again
to hold you once more, as I did then
I only ask, just like before
you could just hold me, so I would feel "more"
you brought me everything
I could want
you held me closer, so that I have not
ever again, been able to find
the peace that I found, when you were mine.

He is by your side

He is by your side

if you should need him

right behind you—

if you don't . . .

in times of trouble

look around—

you will find you're not alone

I don't

I don't even know, where you were then
but I remember, there was a time when
all that I needed, I looked no more
now all I can feel, is your love from before
there's been no other, that I know who'd
have the knowledge and power, to do what you do
somehow I needed, all that you've given
all that you shared, and promised to bring
it's not what you said, that I surrendered
but those that you didn't—the words I remember
all words unspoken, leave me to search

in my own heart

to erase the hurt

perhaps you had never, meant to do this
but all of my life, I will spend missing

not only you

but what you stood for

a window to life

a new open door

the passage to freedom

and ways to become

more than I am

by just being "one".

to never let go

to never let go
to hold on to hope
to always be sure
that I should know
to keep you with me, I'll always be
watching over you
as you did for me
you gave me your hand
so I could stand tall
for when I needed—you gave me all
and anything I wanted
you would have made
so that I'd know, your love remains
whenever the load, became too much
you would be there, with all of your love
you would insist, on taking my weight
so that, if ever
you need back, what you gave
I'd gladly share, all that you bring
now that we know, more than anything
what you had done, you were never alone
for God was behind you
all the way home.

when LOVE gives you wings . . .

when Love gives

      you wings . . . (what that means)

1.   reaching out
2.   taking a chance
3.   getting the facts right
4.   remembering to dream
5.   trusting your heart
6.   talking it out
7.   learning to forgive
8.   identifying barriers
9.   knowing what you want
10.   finding what you need
11.   remembering what to forget
12.   having faith to believe
13.   accepting destiny
14.   learning from the past
15.   eliminating regret
16.   leaving your baggage behind
17.   practicing patience
18.   fine-tuning expectations
19.   preparing to work at it
20.   being grateful for today

PLANNING FOR A BETTER TOMORROW.

Bonus Tip: always read the fine print !

from this day forward

from this day forward, as vows are exchanged
expect that your lives, will not be the same
today's the beginning, of a new life together
enjoy what love brings, when love is "forever"
though "forever" and "always", will not be enough
time to be able, to show all your love
while needing your other half, to be whole
love has a way, of making you grow
kindness, compassion, honesty, and trust
let peace rule your house, along with your love
enjoy the wonder and joy, that your love will bring
if you check with your hearts
that would be "everything"
of all the things, that your two hearts will
want are "forever" and "always"—but still
each day that you love, treasure it more
for each day that you have
is one more, than before
so for "always" and "forever", now you belong
may love make you dream, and your love go on
for a love, that was always "meant to be"
will last your whole lifetime, when one becomes "we".

for the hope

that you

bring my tomorrow

I will always

be grateful

I can't help

I can't help the way, I love you now
it calls to me, and then somehow
it won't let go, it's always there
to remind me, that you are somewhere
I should be, that as your friend
to always have, no matter when
or what you need, just call for me
and I'll be there, as long as we
both still feel the way, that I
have loved you from that moment

time

cannot erase the pain of loss
but what I felt, was just so much
all at once, the smile I knew
the love I wanted, to be true
the way you looked at me, to say
that you'd be back, for me some day
I couldn't move, to say a word
but if you could, you would have heard
the way my heart then, woke up to
want the way, that I want you
I never meant, to tell you this
but I guess now, that I must listen.

a candle

like a candle burning bright
the way you held me, our last night
it flickered once, and then held true
to keep the memory, of you
close to my heart, where you belong
this love I feel, goes on and on
to tell me that, so many times
I needed someone, in my life
to say the words, that you had said
to hold me, just like you did—when
you couldn't know, just what it meant
to feel the love, that I felt then
for now it lives, and teaches me
a different way, the world to see
one full of light, and so much love
how could it be, with just one touch
that now my heart, says it believes
it wants to learn, all that you teach
who you are, and what you need
the way, you open eyes and mind
to feel all things—if you were mine
I'd never need, or want if then
you'd give your heart to me, again.

when "tomorrow"

becomes "yesterday"

we understand

what happened "today".

what happens

what happens next, I do not know
I only want, the love I hold
and keep for you, deep in my heart
to be all yours—while we're apart
I need to send you, all my words
so your heart knows, what mine has heard
and if only, you could hear the way
the things, I know I need to say
you might even run, to hide a while
until your heart, can then decide
but I won't run away, this time
though my heart tells me, I should try
it only wanted, that you could stay
all that I felt, on that last day
was what you brought me, to believe
in love and trust, that makes me need
if you ever think, that I don't care
you need only read, what I've written here
now all at once, and just for you
I want you to know, these words are true
for I always thought, I'd love again
but not the love, you brought me then.

you

you held me close, and then let go

as if you didn't, need to know

the answers, to the questions I

have always had, deep in my mind

if only, you could feel the way

I've kept your love, when you went away

the arms that held me, longer then

I couldn't wait, to feel again

the eyes that held mine, to their own

the way they knew, that they were home

now and forever, and after that

I know once more, I can't just forget

the one whose love, would be for me

for when you came, I began to dream

now all I want, is when you'll next

hold me again, and only then

will my heart say, that it's time at last

to love the one, who has come back

yet there I go, again to dream

of love, and all that you brought me

if I close my eyes, and you're still here

I'll know I can believe

for all I've ever wanted was, to hold you in my dreams.

when

LOVE

gives you

WINGS

"After" Thought

if there was ever any advice

to give

it would be, to follow your heart

for it knows where to go—

you just have to learn

to follow.

Acknowledgements

As I started to write out my list of "I.O.U's", the most important person I would have thanked, told me I should acknowledge "others" first.

That left me with a profound sense there is a Higher Power seeking to work through all of us, if we could only learn to "listen".

That is our job. To "hear" properly, one must "listen" to qualities of "humility" and "understanding". They are related to "kindness" and "equity".Some degree of "anticipation" and "determination" are required.

You will be quite deaf, if you invite in "dishonesty" and "selfishness". And we all need to take a deep breath in between "wanting" and "needing".

I hope that reading "when Love gives you wings" will enable your heart to grow bigger, so it can hold all that it desires.

Seek to acknowledge the role of "patience" and "understanding". They stand quietly by your side until allowed to participate.

"Love" always and forever, reliable and as enduring as memory allows can survive the most hostile surroundings and live beyond what we can see.

You may not recognize love at first, which is why you must treasure it whenever you find it.

This book was written in memory
of all those who have made us love them
and to acknowledge the ambivalence of remembering.

About the Author

The author currently
lives in Mississauga, Ontario, Canada
with her third husband and three children.
Receiving a diploma from the
Institute of Children's Literature
has opened the door to
pursuing self-expression which can make a difference.

Life is all about loving,
losing
then learning to love again—
discovering also, that
life is best lived, when we
choose that which we love
hoping somehow
it will love us back
and even if not,
loving regardless.

It is in loving
that is shared
we seek and obtain redemption.

A previous book

by Gwen Editin entitled

"When you Lose the One you Love"
chronicles the many emotions
that accompany the loss of a loved one
and refers to
"Ten Golden Rules for Life after Loss".

In a subsequent book entitled
"When Love is a New Beginning"
she takes the reader on a journey
that stresses the importance
of remembering
what not to forget.

This book was written
for those who asked
for **"another"** one.

"Life's struggles teach us who we are."

"Life's triumphs confirm who we have become."

Her Motto

"to think, before you speak

to feel, before you write

to know, before you love"

is free to everyone.